Georgia

Money and Me

Christina Hill, M.A.

Consultants

Regina Holland, Ed.S., *Henry County Schools*
Christina Noblet, Ed.S., *Paulding County*
School District
Jennifer Troyer, *Paulding County Schools*

Publishing Credits

Rachelle Cracchiolo, M.S.Ed., *Publisher*
Conni Medina, M.A.Ed., *Managing Editor*
Emily R. Smith, M.A.Ed., *Series Developer*
Diana Kenney, M.A.Ed., NBCT, *Content Director*
Torrey Maloof, *Editor*
Courtney Patterson, *Multimedia Designer*

Image Credits: pp.2,5 North Wind Picture Archives;
pp.2,10 CARLO ALLEGRI/REUTERS/Newscom; p.7 Kristoffer
Tripplaar/Alamy Stock Photo; p.11 Manchester Daily
Express/Getty Images; p.12 Ingram Publishing/Newscom;
p.14 Grant Heilman Photography/Alamy Stock Photo;
p.16 Marc Hill/Alamy Stock Photo; p.16 Brian Alpert/Getty
Images; p.18 Fancy Collection/SuperStock; p.25 KidStock
Blend Images/Newscom; p.27 Peter Glass/Newscom; p.29
Purestock/Getty Images; p.29 Jason Getz/MCT/Newscom;
p.32 Historical Documents Co.; All other images from
Shutterstock and iStock.

Library of Congress Cataloging-in-Publication Data

Names: Hill, Christina, author.
Title: Georgia : money and me / Christina Hill, M.A.
Description: Huntington Beach, CA : Teacher Created
Materials, 2016. |
  Audience: K to Grade 3.? | Includes index.
Identifiers: LCCN 2015042501 | ISBN 9781493825622
(pbk.)
Subjects: LCSH: Finance, Personal--Juvenile literature.
Classification: LCC HG179 .H4695 2016 | DDC 332.024-
-dc23
LC record availab le at http://lccn.loc.gov/2015042501

Teacher Created Materials

5301 Oceanus Drive
Huntington Beach, CA 92649-1030
http://www.tcmpub.com
ISBN 978-1-4938-2562-2
© 2017 Teacher Created Materials, Inc.

Table of Contents

Money, Money, Money!

Long ago, nothing was for sale in Georgia. But people still needed things. They had to **barter**, or trade, for them. Trade was how they got the things they needed.

Today, people in many countries do not trade. They use bills and coins. Bills and coins are called **money**. Money makes it easy to buy and sell things.

Let's Make Money

In 1792, the U.S. Mint was created. It makes all the money used in America. Today, the U.S. Mint prints money using a giant printing press.

Buying and Selling

People today have a system of buying and selling things with money. This is called an **economy** (ih-KAHN-uh-mee).

Some people make goods to sell. Goods are things. These things can include food, clothes, games, and books. Other people sell work that they do. This is called a *service*. Fixing a car is a service. Painting a house is a service, too.

Plenty of Peanuts

Peanuts are goods. Georgia sells more peanuts than any other state!

Zippers are goods made in Marietta, Georgia.

Dog walking is a service.

Producers are people who make and sell things. **Consumers** are people who buy goods and services. Most people do both.

Have you ever been paid to do a job? Maybe you get paid to walk dogs or rake leaves. You are selling a service. This makes you a producer. Have you ever bought new clothes or paid to get your hair cut? This makes you a consumer.

SHOP Online

Buy It Online

Lots of consumers buy things online. This means they use a computer to shop.

Not Enough

There is a limit to how many goods and services are for sale. This is called **scarcity** (SKAIR-suh-tee). Some items can be scarce at certain times.

Lots of people buy toys during the holidays. Perhaps there is a toy that many kids want to buy. The toy might sell quickly. It might even sell out! This means there is not enough for everyone.

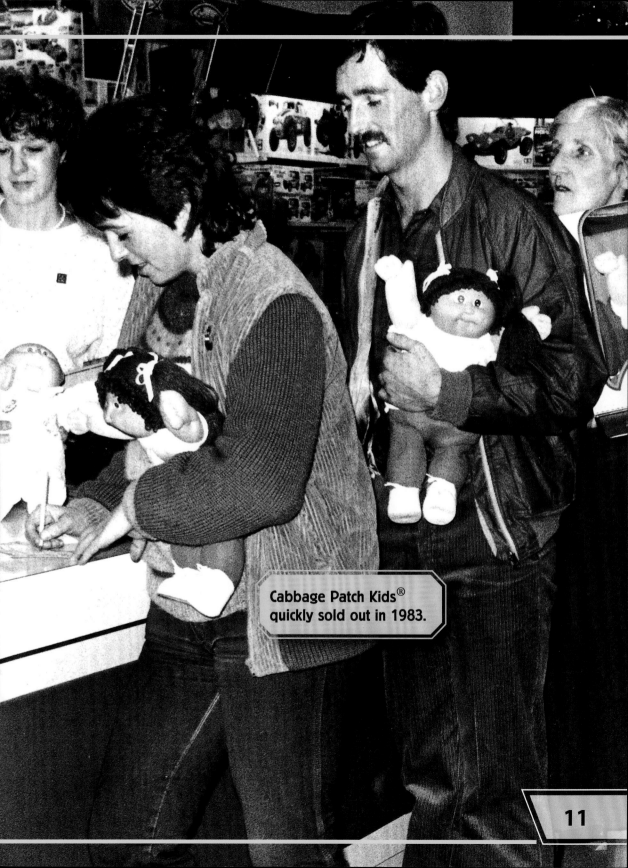

Cabbage Patch Kids® quickly sold out in 1983.

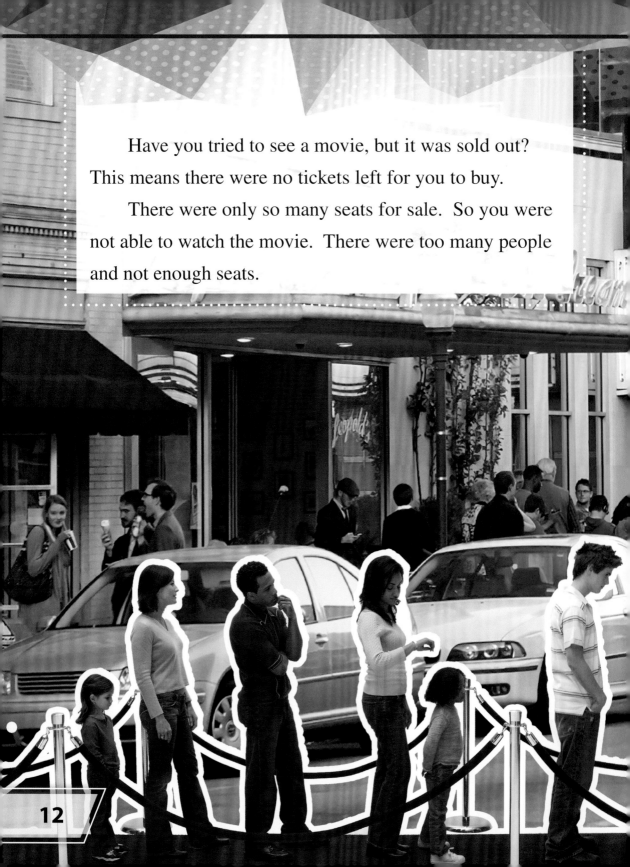

Have you tried to see a movie, but it was sold out? This means there were no tickets left for you to buy.

There were only so many seats for sale. So you were not able to watch the movie. There were too many people and not enough seats.

Supply and Demand

At times, goods are plentiful. Peaches grow better in the summer. This means the **supply** of peaches is high.

Peaches are scarce in the winter. The supply is low. But the **demand** may still be the same. The demand is how many people want to buy that good.

peach orchard in winter

14

Supply and demand can affect the cost of goods and services. Prices will drop when the supply is higher than the demand. But if the demand is high, then the price will rise.

Supply and demand can change over time. That is why prices go up and down.

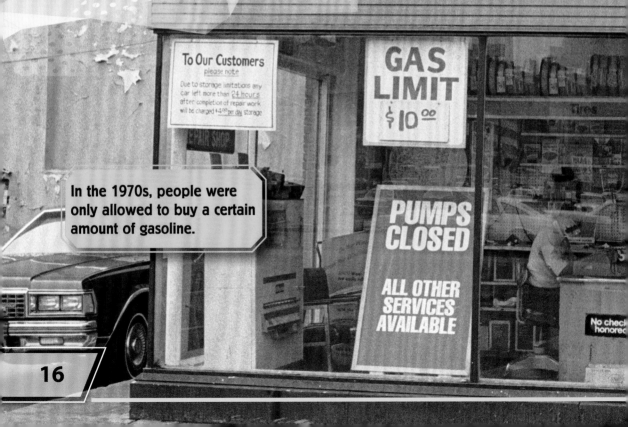

To Our Customers
please note

Due to storage limitations any car left more than 24 hours after completion of repair work will be charged $4.00 per day storage

GAS LIMIT $10.00

Tires

PUMPS CLOSED

ALL OTHER SERVICES AVAILABLE

No check honored

In the 1970s, people were only allowed to buy a certain amount of gasoline.

Super Sale

A good is on sale when the price is lower than usual.

Give It Up

We may want many things. But we may not be able to have all the things we want. We have to make choices.

There are many ways for you to spend your money. You will have to choose to give some things up in order to get other things you want.

Pretend you need new school supplies. You have 10 dollars to spend. You need a new backpack. But you also want some new markers. Both items cost 10 dollars.

You decide to buy the backpack. You don't buy the markers. This is your **opportunity** (ahp-puhr-TOO-nuh-tee) **cost**. It is the choice you give up. You pay money for your choice. You also lose out on what you can't buy.

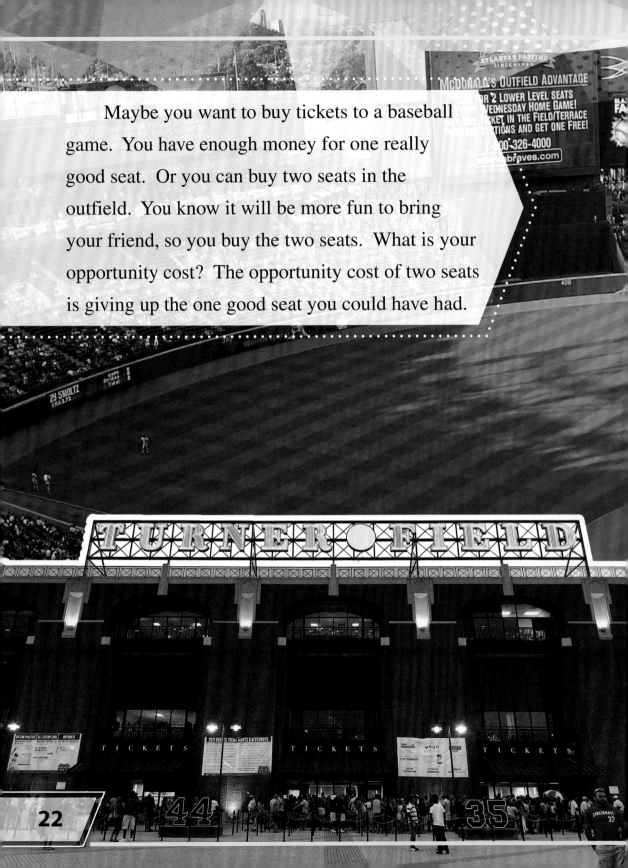

Maybe you want to buy tickets to a baseball game. You have enough money for one really good seat. Or you can buy two seats in the outfield. You know it will be more fun to bring your friend, so you buy the two seats. What is your opportunity cost? The opportunity cost of two seats is giving up the one good seat you could have had.

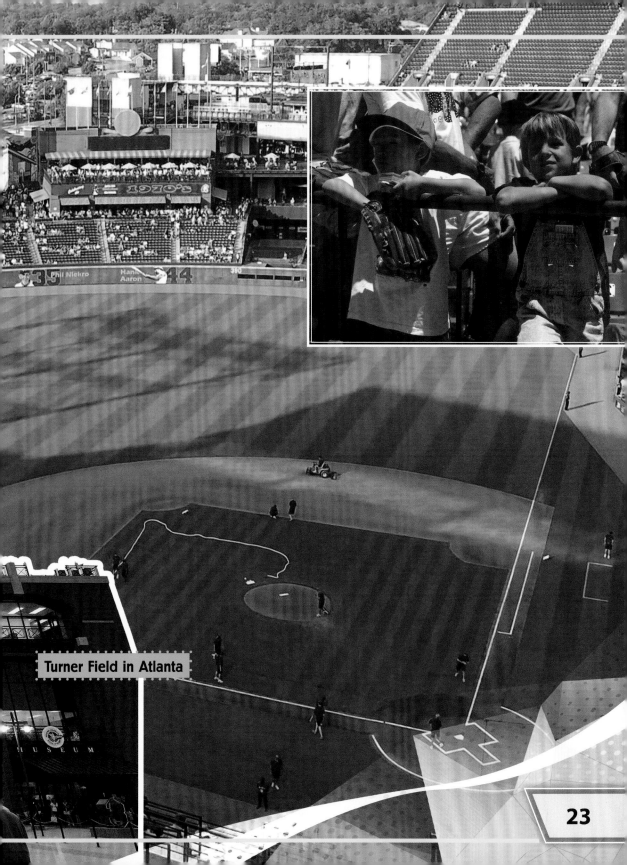

Turner Field in Atlanta

Set Your Goals

It is important to set goals to keep track of your money. A spending plan is called a **budget** (BUHD-juht). Start with how much money you earn. Then, you can make a list of the things you need and how much they cost. This will help you know how much money you have to save.

This boy saves his money at a bank.

Watch Your Spending

You always want to make sure you spend less money than you earn.

Wise Choices

Earning money is hard work! You don't want to spend all your money right away. You will be in **debt** (DET) if you spend more than you earn. To be in debt means you owe someone money.

Save your money. Stick to your budget. Spend wisely. This will help you be a responsible part of the economy.

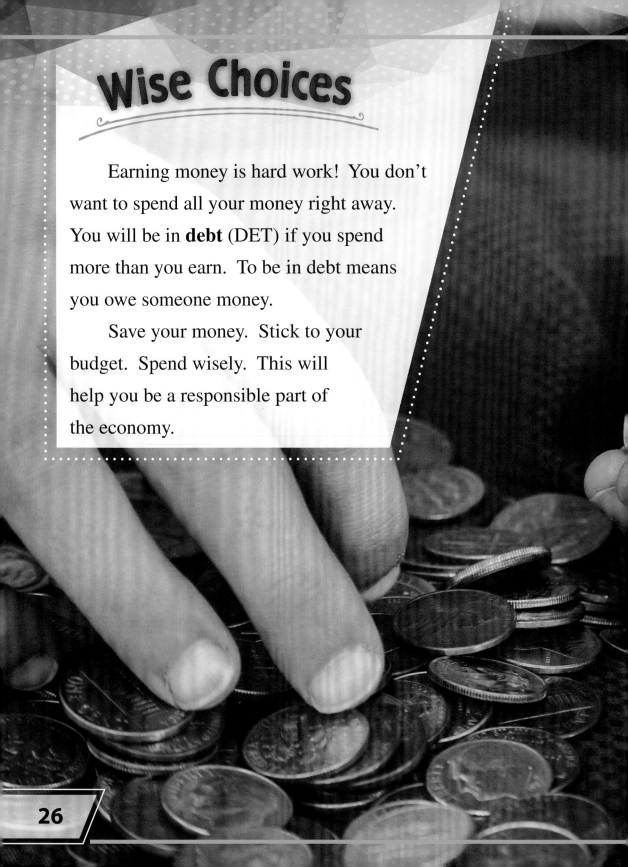

Being Helpful

You can also donate your money to help people in need.

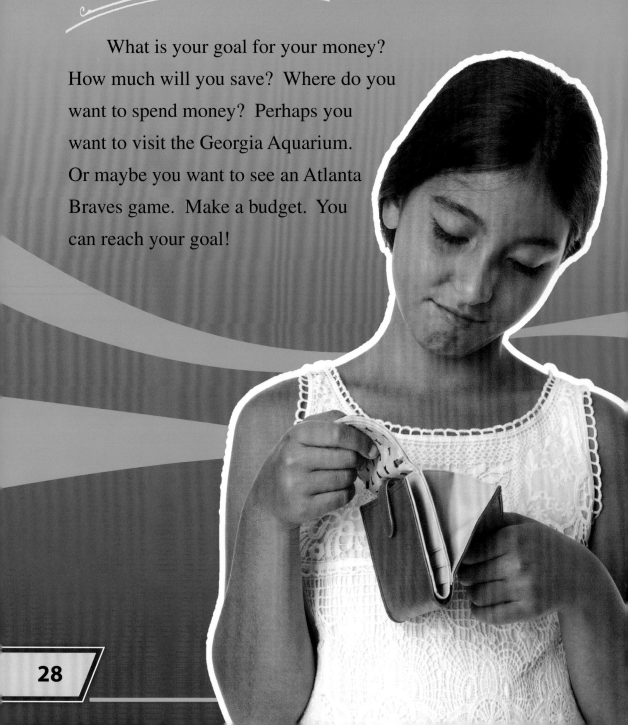

Budget It!

What is your goal for your money? How much will you save? Where do you want to spend money? Perhaps you want to visit the Georgia Aquarium. Or maybe you want to see an Atlanta Braves game. Make a budget. You can reach your goal!

Glossary

barter—trade things for other things instead of for money

budget—a plan for how to spend an amount of money

consumers—people who buy goods and services

debt—the amount of money owed to someone

demand—the need to buy goods and services

economy—the system of buying and selling goods and services

money—coins and bills used to pay for goods and services

opportunity cost—the value of the next best choice

producers—people who make goods and provide services

scarcity—a small supply of something

supply—the amount of goods and services for sale

Index

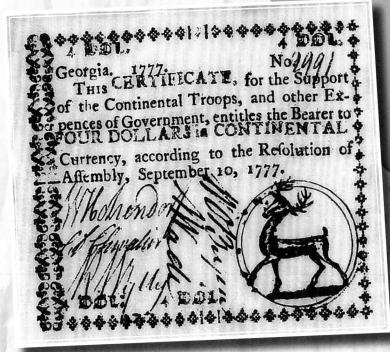

This CERTIFICATE, for the Support of the Continental Troops, and other Expences of Government, entitles the Bearer to FOUR DOLLARS in CONTINENTAL Currency, according to the Resolution of Assembly, September 10, 1777.

Georgia. 1777.

Making Money

Money has looked different ways over the years. How is colonial money different from money today? How is it the same? Decide what is most important to show on money. Then, design your own play money.